D0717512

USBORNE BIBLE TALES

The Christmas Story

Retold by Heather Amery

Designed by Maria Wheatley

Illustrated by Norman Young

Language consultant: Betty Root

Series editor: Jenny Tyler

This is Mary and Joseph.

They lived a long time ago in Nazareth. Joseph was a carpenter. Mary was expecting a baby soon.

They went to Bethlehem.

Mary and Joseph had to walk most of the way.
They had to register to pay their taxes.

Bethlehem was full of people.

Mary and Joseph tried to find a room to sleep in.
But everywhere was already full.

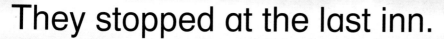

They stopped at the last inn.

"All my rooms are full," said the innkeeper, "but you can sleep in the stable, if you like."

The stable was warm and clean.

Joseph made a bed of straw for Mary. He covered it with his cloak. Mary lay down. She was very tired.

That night her baby son
was born.

Mary called him Jesus. She put him in clean
clothes and made a bed for him in a manger.

Near the town were some shepherds.

They slept near their sheep to guard them from wild animals. It was very quiet and dark that night.

Suddenly, there was
a bright light.

The night sky was filled with light. The shepherds
woke up with a start. They were very scared.

An angel spoke to them.

"Don't be afraid. Go to Bethlehem. In a stable, you will find a baby who is Christ the Lord."

The shepherds went to Bethlehem.

They soon found the stable and knelt in front of the baby. They told Mary what the angel had said.

The shepherds were very happy.

They told everyone in Bethlehem about Jesus.
Then they went back to their sheep, singing to God.

Far away were three Wise Men.

They saw a very bright star moving across the sky.
It meant something special had happened.

They followed the star.

After many days, it stopped over Bethlehem. The Wise Men knew they had come to the right place.

The Wise Men found Jesus.

They went in and saw Mary with her baby. They knelt down and gave the presents they had brought.

Mary and Joseph went home.

They took baby Jesus on a very long, hard journey.
At last, they were back home in Nazareth.